Be Amazing

Tools for Living Inspired

Erin Ramsey

Be Amazing: Tools for Living Inspired

Printed in the United States of America

General editing: Connie Gorrell
Author photo by Daniel Knight, Studio B Photography

OptiMystic Press, Inc.
P.O. Box 6, Woodburn, IN 46797
www.optimystic.press

If unable to purchase this book from your local bookseller, you may order directly from major online bookstores or via the publisher's website.

ISBN-13: 978-0692634660
ISBN-10: 0692634665
Library of Congress Control Number: 2015912531

DEDICATION

This book is dedicated to
Doug, Ryan, Luke, Jack and Molly.

Happiness is the journey, not the destination.

—BEN SWEETLAND

TABLE OF CONTENTS

WITH ABUNDANT GRATITUDE TO:

My best friend, husband and biggest champion, Doug.

My most beloved gifts and greatest teachers my children: Ryan, Luke, Jack and Molly.

My granddaughter Isabelle for bringing such joy and my daughter in law Sam for enriching our family.

My phenomenal niece: Sierra, for editing and contributing to this book and for her courage to sail from the harbor.

My friends for being sounding boards, editors and totally fun; Becky, Kim, Holly, Jen, Tom and Krista. And to all of my POW WOWS!

My mom, my dad and my stepmother, Bev for always telling me I could be what I wanted to be.

My sister Kelly, and lifelong friends Michelle and Michelle, for always having my back.

My brothers, Tim, who I carry in my heart every day, and Tom for planting seeds in my mind about personal growth at a young age.

Grace Winiger and Rachel Wambach for designing the *Living Inspired* flower.

Molly for inspiring the title of the book by hanging a sign on my ceiling fan.

All of the amazing people whose paths have crossed mine; you inspire me.

All My Best,
Erin

Introduction

Living an amazing life does not have to be complicated. Do you ever wonder if you are living the life you are meant to live? Do you ever worry that you might not be making the most of life? We often hear of people on their deathbeds wishing they would have lived differently.

Have you had *your* wake-up call yet? I had mine when I stood in the airport and watched my eighteen-year-old son Ryan walk down the terminal to board a flight. Through my tears, I took a good long look at my life and realized there had been too much time wasted on the things that didn't matter. That moment in the airport was my chance to take action before it was too late. It was my time to take action to create the life I wanted, a life that is full of joy, compassion and gratitude.

You deserve that, too—a life that promotes your authentic spirit in a way that leads to joy, instead of crying in regret. This moment is your moment. You are *amazing*—and you can choose to Make IT Happen!

How to Use This Book

With the right tools we can build a life of inspiration. With the right choices we can make our greatest contributions to the world. As you read this book, you will find that it is full of easy to use tools for creating a life of positive energy and love. Each section includes five components to make it easier for you to navigate.

The components are:

1. Tools
2. *Living Inspired* quote
3. Affirmation
4. Action Step
5. Focus on individual tools:
    a) Feelings
    b) Colors
    c) Considerations

If you use these tools you will be equipped to respond to life and take action in new ways. New responses and proactive action can change your life. Events do not define our lives, rather how we respond to events is what has a profound effect on personal happiness and who we become.

We are meant to live inspired, joyous and full lives. As you compile your tools and make your choices you can create a tool belt for lighting up your world. The tool belt for *Living Inspired* is simple.

It has six Choices for you to consider:

1. Embracing Self-Consideration
2. Practicing Courage
3. Creating Joy
4. Being Compassionate
5. Living in Gratitude
6. Focusing on Presence

Each Choice includes tools for you to use anytime and anywhere in order to help you learn the actions to take. Experiment with them. When you find one or two tools you like for each Choice put them in your tool belt. Stay away from thoughts of perfectionism; don't turn this opportunity into a chore. Focus on having fun while responding in new ways. Be ready for quick and meaningful results. Ultimately, *Living Inspired* is about the contribution you are here to make. You will begin to realize what you have to give as you practice using the tools and making the bright choices.

Once I started to develop these six Choices and connect them to everyday experiences I began to brighten every area of my life. I was an overstressed mom of four children, completely exhausted and unhealthy, working very long hours, with a failing marriage, battling unresolved emotions from my youth and limited authentic friendships.

Through the six Choices, I created a life of meaningful and reciprocal relationships, a heart full of joy and an unending sense of empowerment and contribution. I have spoken to thousands of people and have learned that a few realistic and accessible tools can make a world of difference in the way we live. I create good energy for myself and those around me; I am *Living Inspired* and so can you.

In each Choice section I will refer to the *Living Inspired* flower shown on the cover of this book. It is a visual representation and reminder that you have the tools to make choices that will empower you to live an amazing life. The heart in the center represents *you* and the choice to embrace self-consideration.

The petals are different colors representing each choice:

- Practicing Courage: Orange
- Creating Joy: Yellow
- Being Compassionate: Blue
- Living in Gratitude: Green
- Focusing on Presence: Purple

The flower is a simple, bright and colorful symbol because that is what *Be Amazing* is all about. Depending on where you are in life and how you are feeling you can focus on particular choices and use the colors as prompts for using the tools.

The flower is a reminder that you are amazing!

Please consider this book your companion. It is a loving, inspiring and compassionate friend that wants you to live your life without regret or mediocrity. I have created it to be the perfect portable size and suggest you carry it with you. When you are in a moment of need you can use it to fill up your tank or pull out a tool.

Together we can be who we are meant to be and contribute what we are meant to contribute. Let's brighten up our lives so we can light up the world!

CHOICE ONE

Embracing Self-Consideration

> ***Go out into the world today and love the people you meet. Let your presence light new light in the hearts of others.*** —Mother Teresa

Children can teach us a lot. When my daughter Molly was nine, we were walking on a beach. The white sand was mixed with small white shells. She quietly leaned over and picked up a shell. It was a super tiny and perfectly shaped heart. I wondered how she could have found this tiny perfect heart among all of the shells, sand, seaweed, and waves. We marveled and I said to her, "You just attract love." Her face lit up. She has since found many hearts, including a Rice Krispy, a frosted flake, candle wax, rocks, steak, potato chip, tree stump, burnt cheese, a leaf and the list can go on and on.

The question to ponder is: How many bowls of cereal have we eaten and never found a heart?

The hearts feel like gentle reminders and bold enforcers of what and who all of us really are. We are all just love. When we are considerate of ourselves and stay centered in our core, our true purpose, our calling—to love and to be loved—we are on the path of *Living Inspired.* Our path and our presence are full of spirit. What we see and what we find is a direct reflection of what we carry in our hearts. How we feel about ourselves is directly illustrated in how we feel about others. Hearts are everywhere…if we free ourselves to see them.

Be Kind to the Captain

Self-consideration is not ignoring reality; it is reframing experiences so we can perpetuate self-love and learning.

Embracing self-consideration is the foundation of filling yourself with spirit. It is built upon love. You are the Captain of your ship. The way you see yourself and regard yourself is the measurement in which your life is unfolding. Think about being on a ship. How do you treat the Captain? You would probably treat the Captain respectfully and kindly. The Captain is the one you trust to get you where you are going. We can learn to trust ourselves and treat ourselves with kindness with the right choices and tools. Being kind to the Captain and embracing consideration and responsibility for yourself is the first choice you get to make on the journey to *Living Inspired.*

If you have a tendency to think or say negative things about yourself, please STOP. Nothing good can come from this. It is a waste of time and energy. Actually, it is selfish because it takes away from what you could be doing to help yourself and others.

One simple way to get away from negative self-talk and judgment is to build in a new nighttime ritual. I suggest this because so many of us lay awake rehashing the perceived bad stuff and how we failed in one way or another. So as you lay down tonight decide that if you start thinking about your shortcomings or things you are worried about that you will tell yourself, "**STOP**." Say it boldly and consistently.

Create a picture in your mind's eye. You may want to use a stop sign, the pink heart in the middle of the *Living Inspired* flower, a ship or a picture of you wearing a captain's hat. You can also play water sounds and visualize yourself navigating through the water in a peaceful, loving way. By using a word, a picture or a sound, your new ritual will take hold faster.

Once you stop yourself from sliding down the slippery slope of negativity, replace the nightly process with these questions:

- What do I feel good about today?
- What would I like to have done differently?
- What will I do or how will I respond next time?
- Who do I admire? Who inspires me? What traits do they have that I would like to develop?

Be honest with yourself. We all do and say things that we would like to have done differently. We all get into situations that are not what we hoped for. The fact is that once it is done, it is done. You cannot change the past but you can change what you do with it. You can turn it into your favor. Decide if you want to keep giving it negative energy or if you want to learn from it and be grateful for the new knowledge. Once you answer the four questions, breathe deeply and release it; think about what you are grateful for and tell yourself, "Sleep tight, Captain. I love you!"

These questions will help you be proactive in order to guide yourself, just as a Captain guides a ship. Being the Captain means you take full responsibility and know you have choices in how you choose to live. Your thoughts are powerful so be careful how you think about yourself.

> ***Your worst enemy cannot harm you as much as your own unguarded thoughts.*** —Buddha

- ✓ **Affirmation:** I trust myself and love myself. I am the Captain of my life. I am meant to light up the world.
- ✓ **Action Step:** I will tell myself to "STOP" immediately if I begin any negative self-talk. I will focus on love and learning rather than judging.

I Am Not My Job

Self-consideration is letting your spirit guide you, not your roles.

What makes us think that we can perform wonderfully and give freely if we are exhausted and don't even know what we have on hand to give? When we become defined by the roles we play (mother, friend, employee, volunteer, student, daughter, sister or partner) we lose touch with our truest self. While these roles may be reflections and illustrations of the parts of us, they are not who we are. They may give us opportunity to let our spirits shine if we manage our self-consideration well, or they may completely deplete and even make us sick if we begin to believe they are us.

I am committed to my roles and I take great pleasure in the responsibility to my commitments: family, friends, work, and community. It becomes unhealthy when we are lost in the roles. Right before I decided to live inspired, I was so caught up in everything I had to do and everything I had to prove that I didn't even know I was sick. I ended up with a terrible infection that progressed to the point of being dangerous. For months I knew I felt 'off' but I kept plugging along.

Today I look back and realize I was completely delusional in thinking I was being who I needed to be. I was so out of touch with myself and so caught up in roles I was playing that I was killing myself. I had an inflated sense of responsibility for everyone and for everything. I felt the more I worried about my family and the harder I worked the greater my control of outcomes was. I was like a hamster on a wheel, running nowhere. I was lost in my roles because I was attached to achievement, approval, pride, and ultimately letting my ego sail my ship instead of asking my spirit to take the helm.

Often, our miraculous bodies will let us know when we have become unbalanced. When you feel sick, have a stiff neck, chronic headaches, grumpy, angry, crying all the time, insomnia, complaining and anxiety it might be messages from your spirit to reconnect. Of course you should seek professional help if need be, but also seek spiritual reconnection with yourself. Go back to who you are, not what you are doing. If you want your family to be peaceful, you need to be peaceful. If you want to give freely you need to give to you, too. If you want to teach your children to contribute joyfully, you need to do the same. If you want your friends to count on you and trust you, then you need to trust yourself.

If you are tired, sleep. If you are hungry, eat. If you are stressed, relax. If you feel depleted, fill up your tank. Make the decision and create the time to tend to yourself so you can tend to others. It is not possible the other way around. Stop telling yourself that you can't—and realize that you must. Most things, like laundry, an email, dirty dishes, or a dusty table will be there when you are ready.

Give yourself permission to get to know you. The daily reconnection is something you do with yourself alone. It is acceptable to relax and indulge if you choose to enjoy a magazine or television show, but this doesn't count as reconnection time.

Reconnection is time with you—without outside influences. At first, it may feel uncomfortable or even a waste of time because you are distracted and stressed. Give it time; find ways to make it a special ritual. Make it an appointment on your calendar and treat the time as if you are meeting your most admired hero. You are phenomenal. Let your actions and thoughts reflect this fact.

Ideas for reconnection are sitting quietly, taking a walk, observing nature, closing your eyes and following your breath, soaking your feet, smiling at yourself in the mirror, writing down things you like about yourself, lighting a candle, saying a prayer or meditating.

I know it isn't always possible to do exactly what you need when you need it (especially if you are raising young children or caring for aging parents) but begin to practice this when you can.

As you become skillful at realizing your needs and become adept at meeting those needs you will be surprised at how fast your life will fall into place through your decisions, without even realizing you have become good at considering yourself. Begin with baby steps and practice. You are the Captain, you decide. You can choose to navigate instead of letting the winds blow you where they may. Your needs and your spirit are worthy of five minutes or more a day for reconnection with yourself.

One of the greatest moments in anybody's developing experience is when he no longer tries to hide from himself but determines to get acquainted with himself as he really is.
—Norman Vincent Peale

- ✓ **Affirmation**: I care for myself and nurture my spirit so I may authentically care for others. My value is not what I do; it is who I am.
- ✓ **Action Step**: The roles I play are just roles. They do not define who I am. I will take time to reconnect with myself every day.

Best Friend Messages

Self-consideration is learning to be your own friend so you can be a better friend to others.

Whenever you begin judging or doubting yourself ask, "Is this what I would tell my best friend?"

For example, if your friend said something they wished they hadn't said you would probably tell her it was not a big deal and it will be forgotten and that the experience probably will help her learn for future situations. What do we have the tendency to tell ourselves? "I can't believe you said that. You are so stupid. You completely embarrassed yourself and people will never forget what you said." This type of response is all too common. It is an example of how we are not kind to the Captain. This is a total waste of time and completely unnecessary.

Another good way to use this tool is when you are making decisions that you are uncertain about or when you get an inkling that what you are doing may not be the best thing for you and what you really want. It can include dating someone who really is not a good fit, taking a job that is too easy, hanging out with people that are on a path that you should not be on and million other things we do to ourselves because of doubt, loneliness and fear. When we begin to settle is when we need a Best Friend Message: You are worthy. You are capable. You have unlimited potential.

The next time you are harsh or judgmental with yourself remind yourself that you are your best friend. Focus on accepting that you deserve that which aligns with your highest regard. It is tempting to doubt and settle but when we continue to do the same things over and over again hoping for a different result it is called insanity. You can be your own coach. When we begin to practice self-consideration we begin giving to our self in a way that will propel us to give to others.

> ***Every time you are tempted to react in the same old way ask if you want to be a prisoner of the past or a pioneer of the future.***
>
> —Deepak Chopra

- ✓ **Affirmation:** I am most worthy of understanding and support. I am considerate of myself and others.
- ✓ **Action Step:** The next time I get worried or full of self-doubt I will talk to myself as I would my best friend.

Not My Monkeys

> ***Not my circus, not my monkeys.***
>
> —Polish Proverb

We often tell others, especially our children, to be careful who they hang around with. We hope those we love will find people who are encouraging, who are on the positive path, who are kind and trustworthy and who have their best interest as the highest priority. We operate under the assumption that they can choose with whom they spend time. This assumption is correct and applies to you, too. You deserve that which you hope for when it comes to those who you love. It is your choice.

Knowing what we don't want helps us to realize what we do want. The trick is to find out what distracts us, and then to put all of our energy into what we want to manifest in our lives. Assessing the people with whom we spend our time can help us figure out if they either contribute or deplete our special reserve.

This simple proverb can be a very useful tool when you find yourself in or being pulled into drama, gossip, ill will or just simply distracted from what you really want. The circus is the situation and the monkeys are the people. You don't have to join the circus to still care and help; but you don't have to be consumed by it.

If you have family members that are depleting your energy and are unhealthy for your spirit you can set clear boundaries about how often, if at all, you are going to participate. You will still be able to care for those you love but you won't have to live in the circus. If you have friends or acquaintances that you begin to realize are negative, jealous, or dishonest, you can choose if that is where you want to spend your time.

It can be as simple as carefully choosing who you go out with on Friday night, or who you sit by at your child's event, or who to lunch with when you go out with colleagues. Every moment matters; every influence impacts you.

Sometimes friendships need to change and even end. I had a friend for many years. Our children grew up together. As I started to change, I became unable to tolerate how she was often talking badly about others and obsessing about who was doing what in a very nosy and snarky manner. I often felt she may not have my best interest at heart and was pretty certain if she is talking about others then she was also talking about me. I called her to tell her how I was feeling. She cried and told me she never intended to hurt me; nothing was intentional. I knew she wasn't intentionally trying to hurt me but she was. I knew she could not give what she did not have, but I couldn't keep repeating this broken cycle of trust and hurt if I really wanted to live in a different way. She said, as she was crying, "Erin, I would never hurt you intentionally. I did not realize."

Ironically, as I write this and look back over the years I responded, "Exactly, because you don't consider me." It was time for me to consider myself. I wish her the best and if she needs me I will help her. I am always kind and open but I do not have to spend much time in the cycle of hurt. I am not suggesting you walk away from everyone and everything.

Many relationships and situations will change as you change. This is good, but some will not. My suggestion is to be intentional, loving and focused on reciprocal considerations. I am choosing a circus of possibilities with authentic monkeys who consider themselves and me. You deserve this. Choose your circus. Choose your monkeys.

As you begin to make clear decisions and start to redefine where you use your energy and spend your time you may get lonely or feel isolated. I encourage you to push through these feelings because as you begin to focus on new and vibrant living the payoff will be worth it. You may feel left out, judged, rejected and sometimes even feel guilty. It may get worse before it gets better—but *stay the course*.

These are good signs that you are choosing a brighter path; a path full of self-consideration. When you become good at choosing those with whom to spend your time, and who you let influence your actions and thoughts, it is amazing how the right people and situations start showing up in your life. You will have more to give. You will create more authentic friendships and meaningful moments.

Make room in your life for people who will lift you up. Make room for purpose and contribution. Get clear on what you would like to give and what you would like to receive.

Just by thinking about this you are charting a new course. You don't have to save the world by entering everyone else's circus. You can create your own circus full of love and good energy. People can join you. This is contribution and self-consideration.

It is better to be alone than in bad company.
—George Washington

- ✓ **Affirmation:** I have authentic relationships. I am worthy of others' highest regard and I create meaningful moments that allow me to help others see that we can choose a bright path together.

- ✓ **Action Step:** I will not get sucked into negativity, gossip or ill will. I will learn how to create new and vibrant relationships rather than be in a circus that does not allow me to contribute in positive and meaningful ways.

Rewire for Good

With little changes and lots of practice you can literally create a new way of operating your thinking processes toward goodness.

Why do some people see the silver lining while others remain under a dark cloud? Why are some people considerate of themselves and of others while some people are rushing around like a hamster in a wheel with no real regard for themselves or anyone else?

Dr. Rick Hanson, University of California at Berkeley (https://www.rickhanson.net/) suggests that our brains are predisposed toward negativity. The good news is we can rewire our brains to see the good. We do not have to remain shackled in negativity and draining behaviors and there are steps we can take in turning our thoughts around toward positivity.

Here are three simple steps Dr. Hanson has developed:

1. Look for good facts, and then turn them into good experiences.

2. Really enjoy the experiences.

3. Intend and sense that the good experience is sinking into you.

Here are examples from everyday life:

1. I have fresh coffee in the morning. I am so grateful to have access to good coffee.
2. I love sitting with my coffee thinking about my day. I love smelling the coffee and welcoming the new day.

3. I will carry the peace and gratitude and self-consideration of my morning ritual throughout the day to remember that for which I am grateful.

You can step back and get off the fast spinning hamster wheel so you can give yourself a chance to see, feel and accept the good all around you. With little changes and lots of practice you can literally create a new way of operating your thinking processes toward goodness. You can consider yourself by allowing time and giving focus to the goodness in your life. Rewire for good. Life will be *amazing*!

> ***By taking just a few extra seconds to stay with a positive experience–even the comfort in a single breath–you'll help turn a passing mental state into lasting neural structure.***
>
> —Rick Hanson

- ✓ **Affirmation:** I use my mind and my heart to savor and experience good things in my life. I am considerate of myself so I can give more to others. I feel my feelings and I have become predisposed to goodness in my thinking.
- ✓ **Action Step:** I will pay attention to all to the goodness in my life. I will focus my thoughts and feelings on truly experiencing the good and increase my presence throughout the day so I can allow myself to feel it and see it.

Gift Giving

Self-consideration is generosity to self.

How many times would you like to treat yourself to something extra special but do not? How often do you realize or think about what you might like?

Like many women, I used to give to everyone but myself. If I did give to myself it would be the 'less-than' version—the version that I would never give to someone else. For example, the cheaper tennis shoes or the outfit on clearance but if it was one of my children or a friend I would have bought the best. This notion is not about money; it is about self-worth and self-consideration.

I would get a friend flowers if they were feeling down or write a nice card to a family member, but never to myself. Now I often take the time to cut flowers for myself or write myself a nice note. If I want something and I can afford it I try to buy what I really wanted rather than settling for the less-than version. This takes practice if you are the kind of person that is not normally generous with yourself. Start small. It is not the amount of the gift that counts; it is the practice of consideration. It is powerful and symbolic that you are special to *you*. It is an easy to use tool that can shift your perceptions toward love.

You may not know what you like or what you want. This is common for those of us who have become separated from our true selves. You can get reacquainted with your true self by using this tool. One way you can practice is to begin making a list of things you enjoy. The gifts do not have to be grand. These tools are meant to help you take action in new ways, not to complicate your life. You don't need to read into it or make it hard. Just take a step toward considering yourself in a more proactive way. Do not use money as an excuse because many gifts are free or at a very low cost. A few gifts might include new bubble bath, a nap, a movie, a special snack, flowers, a loving note, hand cream or soap, a good cup of coffee or tea, new underwear, a soft nightie or a good book.

If you happen to be someone who gives freely to yourself but not to others, begin the practice of giving to others. This will be a tremendous gift to you in return. Having a balance of generosity is key to self-consideration.

> ***Love yourself first and everything else falls into line. You really have to love yourself to get anything done in this world.*** —Lucille Ball

- ✓ **Affirmation:** I cherish the friendship I have with myself. I nurture this relationship and I know it is important in *Living Inspired.*
- ✓ **Action Step:** I will give myself a special and thoughtful gift or gesture at least once a week.

Embracing Self-Consideration

Feelings:

You may be uncertain which tools to use. A good way to create proactive focus is to use your feelings as a guide. Focus on self-consideration if you are feeling resentful, depleted, and exhausted or like a victim.

Colors:

Colors help us focus and serve as reminders. Wear bright pink and think of the heart in the center of the *Living Inspired* flower. It represents you and the care you deserve.

Considerations:

1. It may feel weird to talk to or intentionally give to yourself at first. This is a normal part of the process. Just give it a try. If you are uncomfortable just smile and know it is a new day for you. It is funny, so let it be funny.

2. Express gratitude every time you have a new thought pattern or response. This will perpetuate the inspiration.

3. You do not have to do everything at once or all of the time. Enjoy experimenting with each tool. This is not about perfectionism or a new program; it is simply about experimenting and practicing new ways to think and behave that are fun and full of self-love.

CHOICE TWO

Practicing Courage

Courage is the first of human qualities because it is the one quality which guarantees all others. —Aristotle

It is the culmination of a bunch of little things that leads us to fear. It is the culmination of a bunch of little things that will bring us back to love.

Think of the people you admire—the ones who walk into a room and light it up with their kindness and love. People that are very passionate and optimistic, those that rarely complain and are considerate of others they are undoubtedly good at being courageous. They have put forth effort, they have practiced and they have been brave. To live a life of dreaming bigger and thinking bolder requires courage.

What does having courage look like? Courage

is not sky diving or cliff jumping, it is much more subtle. Courage is most often demonstrated in all of the small choices we make—such as the choices to love, to act on and believe in what we want, say and to accept how we feel and live from abundance even when it is scary.

For many of us, fear has crept into various facets of our lives that it is barely recognizable, yet we wonder why we are discontent, unhappy, or wake up one day and realize we are living in mediocrity. The good news is that we can practice having courage; we can teach ourselves to be brave.

> ***The best time to plant a tree was twenty years ago. The second best time is now.***
>
> —Chinese Proverb

Stay on the Love Side

Practicing courage leads us to love.

Living Inspired is staying on the love side. If you are feeling in anyway afraid then you have moved away from love in some way. You can practice being courageous with one choice, one tool, and one step at a time.

It isn't really complicated so don't make it complicated. Courage has everything to do with love. When all is said and done, it is not our accomplishments that matter; it is the relationships that are at the core of our existence. Those that have vibrant, reciprocal relationships are able to give freely and courageously. Those who can do this feel good about themselves. We can teach ourselves how to be confident and inspired by practicing courage. Little by little, we can be braver. We will be more confident. We will have more to contribute.

Get in the habit of asking yourself how you are feeling and acting and then assess which side you are on—love or fear. It is essential to create awareness. It is not important how often you go towards the fear side because we are human and that will naturally happen. The most important thing is how fast you recognize it and move back over to the love side.

> ***I will always have fears, but I need not be my fears, for I have other places within myself from which to speak and act.***
>
> —Parker J. Palmer

- ✓ **Affirmation:** I see and feel love in everything I do and think.

- ✓ **Action Step:** I will notice when I am returning to old habits of fear and I will focus on love as soon as possible.

Below are examples but you can add to this list of feelings to help get in touch with where you are.

LOVE	FEAR
joy	melancholy
contentment	boredom
acceptance	judgement
spiritually connected	loneliness
grateful	resentful
accountable	victim
blissful	heavy-hearted
peaceful	angry
considerate	selfish
confident	insecure
courageous	afraid
thriving	mediocre
possibilities	scarcity

Pick a Word

Practicing courage means that we are brave enough to take action to discover and pursue what we *really* want.

Some of the best beginnings start small. Choosing one word is a doable action. Think about what you really want for your spirit—not for your loved ones, your friends or your bank account—for *your spirit*.

Pick any word you want. Think about it and keep it simple yet meaningful. Then write it down on a piece of paper. Make a pretty sign. Put a nice note on your dashboard or on your bathroom mirror. Put it in your mental tool belt. Use it as a guide. If you pick a word and decide it isn't really what you want, simply know that this is your choice—just start with something to explore.

You can pick a word for the year or a word for a month, or a word for a particular situation. When you are faced with a decision, or choosing a response or making plans ask yourself: Will this support what I really want? Does this decision support _____ in my life? If the answer is yes, move ahead. If you are not sure, take a bit longer to think about it. If it is no, don't do it. When no or maybe are not viable options, ask yourself how you are approaching your obligations.

Try to align your approach with your word. For example, if your word is *peace* you say, "I am tired and stressed out and I have to pay the bills and make dinner." You can use your word. "I choose to be peaceful as I make dinner and pay the bills. I need to get these things done and I choose to do them in peace." This is much better than complaining or dreading because when you make proactive decisions about your thoughts you are creating a positive life.

Remember, how you navigate is your choice. Use the word as a beacon of light on a foggy sea.

> ***Vision without action is a daydream. Action without vision is a nightmare.***
>
> —Japanese Proverb

- ✓ **Affirmation:** My choice is ______! I am worth it and I can make it happen.
- ✓ **Action Step:** I will use my word as a guide for navigating my life. I am accountable for, and intentional in, the way I am living. I am the Captain. I am kind to myself and courageous.

Bust Through the Fear Barrier

Practicing courage is making the decision and taking action that can propel your entire life in a matter of minutes.

Expressing a feeling or setting a boundary is scary for many of us. We become vulnerable and we worry we may not be accepted. It takes courage to be honest. A soft and clear honesty is authentic courage. We don't have to be rude or hurtful because when we are honest it is not about anyone except ourselves. In most situations, what you are afraid to share or do will only require you to act for a minute or two to break the barrier of fear.

Once you begin to practice breaking the barrier, little by little being courageous will get easier. You will begin to feel better about yourself. When we feel better, when we have clear boundaries and when we are honest in relationships we will inevitably be able to give more to others. Living in fear is living in absence of love. Courage is a choice that will propel your life and keep you on the side of love.

This tool is a great way to begin practicing courage. Here is an example. I have a friend who is a good listener. As with most people, her greatest strength can easily become a weakness. She may struggle because many people tell her things, mostly bad things, about others or negative situations. While she has learned not to internalize what she hears, she has not mustered the courage to put a boundary on this type of contamination in her life.

To begin practicing, she can create a sentence to use and remind herself that setting this boundary will only take thirty seconds and she can change the whole trajectory of the relationship. She can say, even if she is petrified, "I am uncomfortable when you tell me bad things about others," or "It might be a good idea to talk to them about it." If she could break through the fear barrier, only requiring seconds, people would stop telling her bad things. She could still be a good friend, probably a better friend, because the relationship can be redefined to focus on other things like ideas, possibilities, hopes, dreams, problem solving, support and companionship. The wasted energy would be no more. You can start with small things you are afraid to do for practice. I started in my twenties by going to the movies alone because I was afraid to go; then I started to look for things I was nervous about so I could practice more. It feels great to bust through our fear, in both big and small things.

Trying something new or taking a risk for what we really want is scary, too. I made a deal with my cousin that I would try hot yoga if she worked on a vision for her life. I was so scared to go to hot yoga because I was overweight and out of shape. I sat in my car and had to tell myself that it is only one hour of my life, it will be over and done with it before I know. I ended up loving it. I look back on how scared I was and how just a few moments of courage opened myself up to whole new experience and rejuvenated confidence. I was also so glad that I didn't waste days on end contemplating, dreading, ignoring and obsessing whether to do it or not.

When we bust through the fear barrier we are able to give attention and effort to those things that we really want. Remember when we are focused in this way we ultimately will have more to give to others. It is truly unselfish to be courageous. Practicing courage is proactive for our mind and spirit.

Another handy tool if you are super afraid is to say, "If this is a disaster, if I completely fail, if I am totally rejected, ______ will still love me." You can fill in a friend, a pet, a partner, a relative or your inner self. Keep perspective. Push through the fear.

You have much more to gain by taking a risk and getting out of your comfort zone than you will ever have if you don't learn to stop living in fear. Even if things do not end up the way you wanted you are still ahead of the game. Doing something is better than letting fear control you.

I gain strength, courage, and confidence by every experience in which I must stop and look fear in the face. —Eleanor Roosevelt

✓ **Affirmation:** I am courageous by sharing my heart and spirit in honest and loving ways. I am authentic and capable of doing what I am afraid to do.

✓ **Action Step:** I will move toward love by facing that of which I am afraid. I remember most fear can be conquered in a matter of minutes. I know that as I practice I will become more courageous and confident.

Wouldn't it be great if…?

When we know what we want and we ask for what we want we are opening the doors to be able to contribute more to others.

Most people spend more time planning a vacation or choosing which car to buy than they do thinking about what they want for their life. The epidemic is that we are either thinking too small or not at all about our greatest hopes and dreams. It is scary to dream big and think bolder because we may risk failure, rejection from others or we may be afraid and feel unworthy of what we really want.

The challenge and responsibility is to be courageous so you have more to contribute. The hope is that you don't wake up one day and realize that you never used your gifts to benefit others because you were afraid or to realize you just let life happen to you. You are meant to live abundantly and joyously.

You can start dreaming bigger by answering this question: Wouldn't it be great if…? Answer it over and over again. As you become comfortable with it, start writing down your answers. Free your mind to think and open your heart to visualize outlandish dreams and impossibilities. At first, this tool may bring out feelings of guilt or greed. You may have thoughts such as: We should not ask for more, we should be content with what we already have, I don't deserve more, it will never happen, people will think I am crazy or every time I get my hopes up, I end up disappointed. These are common reactions. Move past your old ways of thinking, you have new tools now to respond to opportunity in new ways. You are courageous. You may have been conditioned to be grateful and content with what you already have. Gratitude is essential but while you begin using this tool to remind yourself that when we know what we want and we ask for what we want we are opening the doors to be able to contribute more to others. If we continue to think small and without vision, the same happens to those we love the most.

When we step out and begin to live courageously we inevitably empower others to do the same. So forge through the negative feelings and practice using this tool. It is truly life-changing.

This is a powerful tool so make sure that you are saying and writing the experiences, relationships, opportunities and things that you *really want*. You can include vacations, profession, contributions, how you spend your time, where you live, who you are with, how you feel, how you look, and what your hobbies are. By using these outward details of how you want your life to look you will be led to the deepest and innermost desires of how you want to feel and what you want to contribute. Once you compile your responses turn them into present and achieved statements.

Use presence, not contingencies. This strategy plants a more powerful and healthy seed. You reap a great harvest when you plant the right seeds in healthy soil and nurture it over time. Your dreams are the seeds, your thoughts and actions are the nourishment and your harvest is living abundantly in every way.

Listed are examples of how you can move from

asking questions to creating achieved statements:

- *Wouldn't it be great if I wrote a bestselling book?*
- *Wouldn't it be great if I lived on the beach?*
- *Wouldn't it be great if I had lots of authentic friendships and attended fabulous dinner parties?*

Include these types of statements in your working vision (present tense and detailed):

- *I have a best-selling book that is helping millions of people.*
- *I have a beautiful beach house where I walk out my back door with my dogs and enjoy the fresh air and peaceful scenery every day.*
- *I host a monthly dinner party with fabulous friends who support me and I support them. Our friendships are authentic and our best interests are a driving force in all we do.*

Once you have your written statements it is a good idea to create a visual cue to help you envision and focus on what you really want. You can print photos, cut magazine images, write words or draw pictures of everything you want, big and small. I suggest you frame it or use special materials so it is a personal treasure.

> ***Never give up on what you really want to do. The person with the big dream is more powerful than the one with all the facts.***
>
> —Albert Einstein

- ✓ **Affirmation:** I dream big and think bold. I am worthy and capable of having what I really want. I believe in the power of my thoughts and actions. I empower others through *Living Inspired.*

- ✓ **Action Step:** I will take time to think bolder and dream bigger about my life. I will expand my thoughts. I will think about and decide what I really want. I will create a written statement and/or a visual cue to remind myself of my greatest hopes and dreams.

Voice Memo to Self

Dreaming big does not mean you are not content. It simply means you understand that possibilities are endless and you are open to them.

As you begin to practice courage and use the tools, it is important to create things that will keep you focused on your biggest and bravest dreams for your life. A written statement about all of what you really want is important and a vision board is great for a visual reminder, but *hearing* yourself say the words is powerful. I wrote my 'picture perfect' life down and recorded myself reading it on the voice memo feature on my phone. Every morning I listen to it. It's about four minutes long. Record what you want yourself to remember and focus on. Keep everything in the present tense and play it often.

It felt weird to hear myself on the recording at first but now I look forward to listening to it every day. When you use these tools it is unbelievable how fast things start to happen. I suggest you date each voice memo, vision board and written statements because sometimes things happen and you don't realize it. It is important to try to realize as things manifest so you can be grateful and inspired.

> ***Your vision will only become clear if you look into your heart. Who looks outside, dreams. Who looks inside, awakens.*** —Carl Jung

✓ **Affirmation:** I am courageous. I listen to my most inner self and let my spirit guide me to the life of my dreams. I live brightly. I light up the world.

- ✓ **Action Step:** I will listen to myself with well-crafted thoughts and dreams. I understand the messages I allow in my mind and thoughts I think perpetuate my greatest hopes and dreams. I believe in unlimited possibilities. I will take action when I am afraid.

Practicing Courage

Feelings:

You can figure out if you should put concerted effort toward practicing courage by using your feelings as your compass. Focus on practicing courage if you feel unfulfilled, afraid, unchallenged, uneasy, taken advantage of, anxious, restless or longing for more.

Colors:

Colors help us focus. Wear orange to remind yourself to be brave. It could be anything from a shirt to nail polish. Visual cues and heightened awareness help you to remember to practice. Think of the orange petal on the *Living Inspired* flower.

Considerations:

1. You may feel totally uncomfortable and even incapable of imagining beyond where

you are. It is okay; you just need to practice new ways of thinking and keep your fear at bay. Just keep using the tools even if you don't totally believe it yet. Before you know it, they will start to work and you will be flabbergasted by the results.

2. You might feel nuts or those around you might tell you are nuts; this is a good sign. It means you are breaking free of old thought patterns and starting to dream bigger.

3. Being afraid and feelings of loneliness by choosing new or redefined relationships is a sign of progress. Remember, if you want something to be different you need to do something different. It might be hard but it will be worth it.

CHOICE THREE

Creating Joy

Joy is the holy fire that keeps our purpose warm and our intelligence aglow.

—Helen Keller

This life is finite but our spirit's love and joy is infinite. It is just as easy to be joyous as it is to be unhappy. Do not wait for good times and lots of laughs to come your way, make them happen every day.

Don't Postpone Joy

Life is short; we are meant to live joyously.

It was a stormy day and I was stuck in the Chicago airport. It was difficult to keep my thoughts positive and my presence peaceful amongst crowds and frustration. Out of the corner of my eye I saw a man's t-shirt that said *Don't Postpone Joy.* It felt like a message to keep trying to stay positive.

I wanted to ask him where he got his t-shirt but he was gone. So I wrote down *Don't Postpone Joy*. Not but a minute later he walks by again; I stopped him. I told him I thought his t-shirt was cool and asked where he found it. He proceeded to tell me that the t-shirts were made in honor of his friend. He shared with me he had a friend named Joy who was killed in a car accident in her twenties. When she was alive she would always say, "Don't postpone joy." They made the shirts for her funeral. Life is short. We are meant to live joyously.

Every moment is an opportunity to welcome joy into your life. By using your thoughts and intentions you can choose where to focus. Things like traffic, bad weather, and negative people are often used as a big distraction and a joy drain. The trick is to focus on yourself and how you perceive each moment and each situation. When you have opportunity to do something fun seize it. When you see something funny let yourself laugh. Keep focused on gratitude and courage and the power you have to make joy a current reality.

Joy is what happens to us when we allow ourselves to recognize how good things really are. —Marianne Williamson

- ✓ **Affirmation:** I live in the moment and I embrace joy in every aspect of my life.
- ✓ **Action Step:** When I get caught up in stress or judgement or sadness I will remember the moment for joy is now. I will no longer postpone my joy.

Break the Bad News Trance

Finding positive ways to nourish your mind creates joy.

The information we let into our minds can be compared to food. If we eat healthy and stay nourished we will be healthier and have more energy. The same goes for what we let into our minds. If we wake up and read positive things and think about contributions we would like to make for the day we are off to a healthier start. If we end our day with proactive self-consideration and positive reading we are nourishing our minds as we go to sleep. Millions of people are actually in a bad news trance and don't even realize it.

Most people wake up, have a cup of coffee and read the newspaper or watch the morning news. They go to work and talk with people about bad stuff on the news or in the paper. They proceed about their day, go home make dinner and watch the evening news, and then the late news. They go to sleep, and repeat this day after day. This is what I call the Bad News Trance.

The research of Dr. Graham Davey at the University of Sussex indicates that negative news makes us sadder and more anxious which is no real surprise. The surprising finding of his research is that our personal concerns are exacerbated by the negative news not just the topics in the news. He refers to this as a cascading effect of watching negative stories. The best thing you can do is to tune out negative news. Many people tell me it is irresponsible and that we need to be informed citizens. We do not need to consistently fill our mind up with information that does nothing other than drown out all of the good ideas, joyful moments and kind acts that could have occurred if we weren't in the Bad News Trance. Try it for a week. Turn off the news and put down the newspaper. If you need or want to know more, you can proactively pursue the information. Try not to let outside influences pour sensationalized negative things into your life.

If you are worried about missing something important, ask others to let you know if they think you need to know something. If there is a rare occasion of good news that I would like to know about my friends will usually let me know. If you feel uncomfortable then just watch the news long enough to get the headlines, then turn it off. This tool can also be used with social media.

Try to manage your contacts and news feeds so you have mostly positive people and information. For certain, protect the beginning and the end of your day. These are times you need to clear your mind and set the vision for what you really want.

> ***The mind is everything. What you think you become.*** — Buddha

- ✓ **Affirmation:** I treat my mind with respect and fill it with helpful, proactive and positive information so I can contribute more during my life.

- ✓ **Action Step:** I will turn off the news. I will break the bad news trance and replace the time I spend on bad news with good reading material, quiet time and recorded meditations. I will enjoy conversations with those I love about possibilities, ideas and solutions.

Say Yes With a Clean Heart

Saying *yes* with a clean heart is not a free ride to saying *no* to people and situations that have meaning and purpose; rather it is a ticket to stop saying yes out of guilt.

How many things are you doing but in all honesty don't want to be doing? Take a minute and really think about this question. It is important because you may be blocking joy from your life by saying yes as a default response.

Getting in the habit of saying yes, to be open-minded, open-hearted and giving is different than just saying yes out of guilt or obligation. When we say yes out of guilt, the need for acceptance or obligation our giving stifles the possibilities. It is important to learn personal boundaries, get in touch with what you *really* want, what you want to give, and how you can serve by knowing your gifts and talents. Saying yes from a place of abundance will release energy to attract joyful people, experiences and relationships and will lead to an inner peace.

When you are asked to do a favor or task, you will begin to know when to say yes as you practice choosing a clean-hearted response and learn to respect yourself and your chosen path. When you step forward into *yes* it will be genuine, authentic and joyous. If you are only saying yes with dread, guilt or the need for approval or self-importance it is a great challenge, probably impossible, to create joy out of the giving.

When you begin to make choices with a sincere and honest approach people may be annoyed, may even talk ill about you, and may judge you. Remember that this is their reality manifesting; it has nothing to do with you. In fact, it is likely they are doing many things out of guilt or self-importance. An unclean 'yes' is the very nemesis of *Living Inspired.* It drains your spirit.

Sometimes we have to do things we don't always want to do. It may be cleaning, it may be a project at work, or it may be a favor for a parent. Saying yes is often part of our basic responsibilities. This is part of living a full life and doing these tasks are necessary. Once you develop ways of being and responding that are built on joy and abundance the dread will disappear, and since you will be doing less of the other things you didn't really want or need to do, the things you *must* do become less overwhelming or dreadful.

I was standing in my son's classroom at a holiday party when I started to realize that I needed to step back from saying yes out of guilt and the need for acceptance. I was a very busy working mother. I wanted to do it all and be it all, so I rearranged several things at work in order attend the holiday party to help. I stood there (after rushing and shuffling) thinking that my son did not need me there as he was having a blast with or without me. The other mothers were talking about who wasn't there. I realized I did not care to use my time rushing around only to listen to gossip.

I love helping my children and being a part of their lives but there many other ways I could do this. I started to think about how I could show up with a clean heart and focus on contribution and joy, not out of obligation or the need for acceptance.

Over the years we have had thousands of hours of my children's friends hanging around our house, hosting birthday parties, end of school parties, fire pits, sleep overs, conversations and meals. My time doing these things created joy. I may not have always been in the 'in crowd' at school with the other parents but I was showing up for my children with a clean heart and lots of fun.

I continue to volunteer but I always check with my heart first to ensure my time and effort is aligned with what I really want—to be there for my children, not to be seen as a good mom or accepted by the other parents. I began to teach myself about making a clean-hearted yes, then future decisions became easier and crystal clear resulting in abundant joy. Just recently, my son Jack said, "Mom, I am glad our family doesn't think it needs to be like other families." His statement is a testament to clean hearted decision making; it is important to teach this to those we love the most.

On the other hand, you may say yes when you don't really want to but you do because it is aligned with your values. This is a clean yes. The mother of a close friend died unexpectedly and a few months later my friend called to ask if I wanted to train to walk a half marathon with her. I initially did not want to but after some reflection I said yes. I said yes because I knew she needed me and I wanted to be there for her. It turned out to be a fabulous experience that created much joy.

I learned a lot about myself, improved my health and showed up for a friend. It is important to make your decisions based on what you want and how you want to be even if they are hard. Saying *yes* with a clean heart is not a free ride to saying *no* to people and situations that have meaning and purpose; rather it is a ticket to stop saying yes out of guilt. That serves no one.

You may be doing many things that do not align with what you want in your heart. It might feel like you are sleepwalking; doing and doing more and more. We need to be awake to create joy. Give freely, lovingly and aligned with your plan.

As you begin to check in with yourself you can use these reflective questions to guide your decisions:

- Is this something to which I can contribute?
- Is this something that will help someone I care about?
- How will I feel if I say yes?
- Will this opportunity allow me to share my gifts and talents?
- Am I seeking acceptance and freedom from guilt by saying yes?

Create a world in which it is easier to love.

—Freire

- ✓ **Affirmation:** I say YES with a clean heart. My giving comes from joy and abundance. My contributions are guided by my heart and spirit. I know how to give freely and live lightly.
- ✓ **Action Step:** I say YES when I can give the most from my spirit. Guilt and obligation will not guide my decisions. I will step back and check with myself before I say yes.

Good Morning, Good Looking

Smiling creates presence; presence brings joy.

You can build a habit of greeting your daily routines with joy. One of the first steps in creating more joy is ensuring your mood is good. Practicing and intentionally smiling at yourself and others is an essential tool for improving your mood thus creating joy. Building a smiling habit throughout your daily routines will bring a 'top of mind' awareness to how you are feeling and what you are projecting. Both of these things are directly related to how you are living and what you are welcoming into your life. If we want more joy and we want to be *Living Inspired* it is essential to feel good and be open. Smiling is a catalyst for these things.

Every morning, get up and say out loud or in your mind, "Thank you for another day." Walk into the bathroom and while you are putting toothpaste on your toothbrush, smile and say out loud or in your mind while looking straight into your eyes in the mirror, "Good morning, good looking!" Do this even if you are exhausted, stressed out or dreading the responsibilities of the day. This habit will help you change the way you navigate for the rest of the day, day after day, which makes up your life. Depending on your mood you may think it is funny or you may think it is the stupidest thing ever. It doesn't matter what you are thinking, do it anyway; build a new habit in the morning. Slap on a big smile, wink, give yourself thumbs up, make eye contact with yourself and greet your spirit and your day in a new light.

Find other opportunities to smile throughout the day. When I get in the car I smile and wave at others. When I enter a store I smile, when I go into a meeting I smile. I need to remind myself. Smiling becomes a habit once you begin to build into your daily routines. It feels better than being distracted by what I need to do or consumed by my thoughts. Smiling creates presence and presence brings joy.

Learning to manage our moods and to use our feelings as our guide is essential to creating joy. Another way I like to alter my mood to the side of love is with music. I created a playlist for the sole purpose of lifting my mood. Make a good mood playlist.

Think about which songs make you want to sing and dance and smile. It may take a while or you can build it as you hear songs you love. Embark upon making a joyful playlist by being intentional. Use tools to manage your mood.

The most important decision you make is to be in a good mood. —Voltaire

- ✓ **Affirmation:** I set the tone for each day. My joy comes from within and shines out to the world bringing light to others. I am enthusiastic and know what makes me feel good.
- ✓ **Action Step:** I will smile throughout the day. I will greet myself with a positive statement, a smile and eye contact each day because how I treat myself is how I will treat others. The joy I create is my choice. I will be aware of my moods and I will take steps to become joyous. I know that even if it feels like it isn't working it's moving me in direction of *Living Inspired.*

Make Up Good Stuff

Save your bold energy for love.

We often listen to our thoughts too much. Our thoughts are most driven by ego telling us things to make us feel important, or right or powerful. In another reality, a reality created by love and driven by joy, our thoughts tell us very different things; things that are focused on accepting others, giving the benefit of the doubt, seeing the good and having peace. Basically, we make up stories and begin believing them without evidence. My theory is if we are going to make up stuff we should at least make up good stuff.

Step back for a moment and think about a time when you thought something occurred or someone did something to hurt you or deceive you but once you learned more about it you realized you were wrong. You did not have all of the information which resulted in your ego telling your spirit to protect, get defensive, and see the bad. Think of the stress and time you wasted, the joy you blocked from your life for absolutely no reason other than you believed your story; the story your ego gave your mind. The goal is to replace the untrue, invalidated negative stories with the possibly untrue, invalidated funny and happy stories. Most of the stories in our minds are untrue and invalidated you might as make them good ones.

Usually when people get cut off on the road while driving they will snarl, flip the bird, yell or feel stress in their body. This is a total waste of energy but a knee jerk reaction of the ego. Your job is find tools to interrupt these knee jerk reactions. When something happens to me on the road I say or think, "They must be in labor," or "their friend or wife is in labor." Who wouldn't make room and exceptions for welcoming a new baby? My husband will often say or think, "Oh, they must be getting ready to poop their pants." Who doesn't empathize with that situation? The fact is you were cut off for reasons you don't know. They may be a jerk—all the more reason to send positive energy.

Most likely they may not have seen you, if it was your friend you probably would have justified it for them so why not a stranger? We are all one and you are doing yourself a favor.

Other times we make up stories when people are rude or are takers instead of givers. My mental response is they must have unmet needs. People who act in unloving ways usually have unmet needs. We all have unmet needs; we all have moments when we are not our best selves. Send out what you want to receive in return. This creates joy in your life.

You can even start having fun contests with your family and friends about who can make up the best and funniest stories for situations out of their control that may have caused negative feelings in the past. Start a 'make up good stuff' contest. Imagine if we talked about that instead of all of the perceived bad stuff that happened. Choose to create joy.

I am not suggesting we increase our delusions or ignore situations that must be addressed. I am suggesting that we navigate the sea of life with a new compass; a compass guided by love. One that, when possible, will help stop us from creating bad stories and create good ones (especially in instances when you might regularly let a very small happening ruin your moment, or your day or your week). Save your bold energy for love.

> ***If you are not taking responsibility for your state of consciousness, you are not taking responsibility for life.*** —Eckhart Tolle

- ✓ **Affirmation:** I see good and humor in every situation and everyone. I use my actions and thoughts to create more joy. I am aware of my thought patterns and use my spirit of love to guide me in all situations. I create joy.
- ✓ **Action Step:** I will stop knee jerk, ego driven reactions and judgments by replacing them with funny and happy thoughts. I will focus on joy. I know that I have the power to choose to create joy in my life.

Laugh on Demand

You can make your own funny; you don't have to wait for funny people or funny situations. Laughter is your spirit shining. Shine bright.

There is a plethora of research on how healthy laughing is for the body and the mind. Laughing gets your blood flowing; it releases endorphins, relaxes your body and boosts your immune system. Laughing gets us in a better mood and inevitably spreads joy to those around us. We all like a good laugh but most of us wait for something funny to happen or for a funny thought to come to mind.

About twenty years ago I saw a story on television about a laughing club that would meet to laugh together. I tried to make myself laugh by making funny noises and fake laughing sounds—all by myself. It worked. I looked in the mirror and literally cracked up! I started doing it with my children and their friends and it works for most people.

We can make our own funny. We call it 'Laugh on Demand.' I use this tool if I am feeling grumpy or negative. It immediately gets me in a better mood. I don't always break out into bold laughter but I always at least smile. I know it will probably feel uncomfortable. This feeling is normal because this is probably a new tool for you. Practice it with yourself and, if you get really brave, do it with others.

Another good way to get you laughing is to watch all of the hilarious videos of animals, situations and babies online. Sometimes if I feel out of sorts I will sit and watch a few of these hilarious videos. A few good laughs changes everything. The trick is to realize that you are not laughing enough and find ways to create your own funny!

> ***There is little success where there is little laughter.*** —Andrew Carnegie

- ✓ **Affirmation:** I make my own funny because joy comes from within. Joy is my choice and I use tools to create more of it. I live full of spirit. Laughter is my spirit shining. I shine bright. I light up the world with love.

- ✓ **Action Step:** I will try Laugh on Demand at least three different times this month. I am brave and open to being uncomfortable because I know I must do different things to create joy. I don't have to wait for it. I will make my own funny.

Effortless Hospitality

You are a catalyst for joy.

Being open to possibilities means not letting little things get in the way of big things. Being hospitable sets your priorities straight. Dusty furniture does not trump laughs with friends. Stacks of laundry do not replace consoling a friend over a cup of coffee. A gourmet meal does not supersede cheese and crackers and a moment with someone you care for. A crowded living room does not overtake a joyful gathering. Light a fragrant candle, clean the toilet and you have no more excuses not to open your heart and your home.

Creating a platform to bring people together is a wonderful way to create energy around positive experiences. There is no perfect time to have a gathering. Your space may not be clean enough, your refrigerator might not be full enough and your laundry might be stacked high but those things are no reasons not to open your home and your heart. I wonder how many opportunities I missed to help someone, to offer a sense of belonging, to create fun times and to share in sorrow because I let my worries and distractions prevent me from opening up myself and my home. Put people first. Go out of your way a bit. Be a catalyst for joy.

Once you begin to welcome people in ways that are aligned with sharing your spirit hospitality will become effortless. You and your home will be a platform for togetherness and joy. You will be happier because you will be focused on what really matters to you.

> ***Things that matter most must never be at mercy of things that matter least.*** —Goethe

- ✓ **Affirmation:** I am open to all possibilities. I open my heart and my home. I am a catalyst for creating joy. My heart guides me and I always put people before things.

- ✓ **Action Step:** I will invite someone to my home. I will make the time special with my presence and I will give what I have to make that person comfortable. I will take action to be open and set my priorities in a way that creates joy.

Creating Joy

Feelings:

When choosing the most useful tools for your tool belt you can be guided by your feelings. Consider using these tools for creating joy when you feel sad, mediocre, melancholy, aggressive, lonely or bored.

Colors:

We can use colors to prompt our thinking and actions. When you want to create joy think of the yellow petal on the *Living Inspired* flower. It is bright, vibrant and shines like your spirit will when you are joyous.

Considerations:

1. Using some of these tools may be stretch for you. Stretching is good. If you want a new way of navigating your life you need to try new things. Smile and greet yourself; remember you need to give to yourself first. A good laugh, a kind smile and a positive affirmation can go a long way. They are worth the awkwardness initially. Don't worry it will all become a new normal for you soon enough.

2. Thinking about choosing your mood might be the biggest challenge because it is the notion of complete accountability. Keep your ego in check; it will probably be telling you that bad things are happening and you can't ignore them. Acknowledge these thoughts then move in the direction of using these tools to create joy. This is the process of freeing yourself and using your spirit to light up the world.

3. We are made up of energy. Being joyous and open leads us to higher energy fields which attracts higher energy people and situations. *Living Inspired* is being on the high energy field.

CHOICE FOUR

Being Compassionate

> ***Love and compassion are necessities, not luxuries. Without them humanity cannot survive.*** —Dalai Lama

Sometimes we experience a moment that changes everything. It is a moment that offers an opportunity to operate on a new level of under-standing that gives us one more sparkle in our heart to shine a little brighter. These are the moments to savor. Compassion does not have to be some huge spiritual journey with years and years of practice or sacrifice. In fact, it is quite simple. All we have to do is to choose to come from a place of love even when we don't understand or agree. The trick is to learn how to be compassionate to yourself first. Choosing to embrace self-consideration is the very foundation of compassion.

Compassion is where consideration of self and others is manifested. It is in our darkest hours, during our greatest challenges and most intense pain, that we learn a deeper level of compassion.

The closer I look at others with an open heart the more I realize that we all want to feel accepted and connected. When we allow ourselves to step back from our own pain and fear we can offer true compassion to others.

Everybody Has a Story

Compassion is when your heart sparkles.

I was walking down a crowded Chicago street with three staff members. We were excited to be in the hustle and bustle while attending and presenting at a national conference. There was a homeless gentleman sitting on the sidewalk so I casually handed him a couple of dollars. One of my colleagues asked me why I gave him money. I didn't really respond and kept walking. I was hoping she would just let it go but she didn't. She kept questioning me and pointing out that he was just going to go buy booze and cigarettes with the money. I didn't want to make her uncomfortable but I needed to respond.

I said, "I have a brother who is homeless and I hope if someone walks by him they will help him even if it is for cigarettes or booze." I had a tear in my eye. As I write this, years later, I have a tear in my eye because it gets to the core of who I am and what I am willing to give when it is my story.

The real work is what we do and what we give when it isn't our story. Evening out the story's value, calibrating our hearts for acceptance and aligning our actions propels us to a new level—a level where our hearts sparkle. When we shine others can do the same. This is born out of compassion for ourselves and for others no matter the story. My colleague did not mean harm, but now I am sure she has a new story the next time she sees someone in need. We can help each other expand our understanding.

We're all just walking each other home.

—Ram Dass

✓ **Affirmation:** I always choose love. My heart sparkles and I shine bright to light the path for others. Everybody really does have a story and things are not always as they appear. Today I open my heart wide and send love to everyone. Nothing else matters.

- ✓ **Action Step:** When I feel judgmental or annoyed with myself or others I will remember that everybody has a story. I will remember that all stories matter. I will expand my view and open my heart so I can sparkle.

Find a Back to Pat

We let who we really are shine brightly when we help another.

On an early morning flight out of my quaint Midwestern airport arose a moment of beauty from one of panic. As we began to taxi out onto the tarmac a woman abruptly came down the aisle to the flight attendant. She told her, "I can't do this." She leaned over the beverage service counter and kept repeating, "Sorry, I'm sorry." As I watched her panic, I prayed for her and sent energy of peace and calm. Tears came to my eyes as I watched her struggle with her fear. She could not possibly withstand being closed in on a small airplane. She tried, but needed to get off before takeoff. She couldn't do it. As I watched, I saw the strangers around her begin to care for her.

The flight attendant patted her back. In a very calm, kind voice said, “Let’s put some air on you.” As she sat down, the man sitting beside her reached his arm up to welcome her to the row, he put his hand on her back and started to make small talk with her, an obvious kindness aimed at distracting her. Moments later the gate agent came running out as the plane door with descending stairs was opened to release the claustrophobic, embarrassed, and panicked lady off the plane.

As she walked down the stairs to her freedom, the gate agent held out his arm and smiled at her. He put his hand on her back, patted it and talked with her as he escorted her back to the terminal. I was moved to tears by three strangers reaching out, touching someone who was suffering.

Do we need to wait for a panic stricken woman on a small plane at a quaint Midwestern airport to reach out a hand and pat a back? Look for ways to help someone. Compassion is beautiful; we grow from it. We let who we really are shine brightly when we help another.

I keep seeing the hands, reassuring voices, and soft smiles of strangers in my mind. Opportunities to pat a back are in front of you every day. Look for them. Compassion is the way. Love is the answer.

Compassion is the keen awareness of the inter-dependence of all things. —Thomas Merton

- ✓ **Affirmation:** The Universe offers opportunities every day to lend a helping hand and learn better how to use my heart as a guide. I see and act on these opportunities to make my greatest contributions during my time on earth.

- ✓ **Action Step:** I will practice reaching out to others when I have a natural inclination to do so. I won't let fear, awkwardness or distraction prevent me from taking compassionate action. I will take action to love myself and others every day.

Plant Seeds of Love

By caring for another living thing we learn to better care for ourselves.

I have a brown thumb and a busy schedule but I always feel great when I take the time to water a plant, talk to my peach tree, prune my lavender plants or pet my dogs. Most of us have many people and activities to tend to in our daily lives. Unfortunately, this 'tending to' becomes rote and even stressful which diminishes our capability to practice being compassionate. We become depleted, exhausted, resentful, numb and even just plain angry at all of the stuff we need to do to keep our families and work on track. This is when we are most off track.

Try to step back a moment. Make a choice that is intentional, filled with presence and a clean heart to nurture something of your choosing. It can be anything, a pet rock, a plant, a seed, a child or a friend. Intentionality is the key here; not what you choose to nurture but how you do it. By caring for another living thing we learn to better care for ourselves. We must be intentional and present in the nurturing process to garner the greatest contribution and growth.

> ***The heart is like a garden. It can grow compassion or fear, resentment or love. What seeds will you plant there?*** —Buddha

- ✓ **Affirmation:** I care for other living things while simultaneously caring for myself. I take time to nurture. I am always planting seeds of love.
- ✓ **Action Step:** I will find a way to nurture something new or in ways that are renewed with

heightened appreciation. I will plant seeds of love through my actions. I will intentionally practice compassion.

Be an Instrument

Make your life a masterpiece of contribution and love.

If you were an instrument what song would you play? If you were a tool what would you build? If you were an author, what story would you write? We can create our own story and our own song. We need only to ask for help and understand that we will get off course. Just keep asking for help and getting back on course. Make your life a masterpiece of contribution and love.

The next time you are leaning toward judgment, annoyance or frustration ask yourself what song your thoughts are creating. When there is an opportunity to help another ask yourself what story you are writing with your actions. Be an instrument of peace, for any other way is not what we are meant to be.

Start by doing what is necessary, then do what is possible; suddenly you are doing the impossible. —Francis of Assisi

✓ **Affirmation:** My life is a masterpiece of love. I give freely. I understand my impact on others is significant. I seek help when I need it because I am humble and strong.

✓ **Action Step:** I will ask myself what song I am playing or story I am writing every day. I will be an instrument of peace and compassion through my thoughts and my actions.

The Peace Prayer

Lord, make me an instrument of Thy peace;
Where there is hatred, let me sow love;
Where there is injury, pardon;
Where there is doubt, faith;
Where there is despair, hope;
Where there is darkness, light;
And where there is sadness, joy.
O Divine Master, Grant that I may not so much seek to be consoled, as to console;
To be understood, as to understand;
To be loved as to love.
For it is in giving that we receive;
It is in pardoning that we are pardoned;
And it is in dying that we are born to eternal life.
~Amen

Do Something

Active compassion is your gift to be who and what you were put here to do and be.

It is surprising how we can become paralyzed. It almost appears to be a slow and insidious process fertilized by criticism, insecurity, social norms or even our own selfishness. It doesn't really matter; what matters is how we free ourselves from stagnant and mediocre navigation of our life into vibrant and thriving action.

I took my three little boys to a matinee. As we were leaving the theater an elderly gentleman tripped down the two stairs leading to the exit. He was lying there; no one was helping him. I ran over to him telling my boys to stay close and hollered for someone to call 911. There were many people around, closer in proximity to him and without the accompaniment of three small boys to manage, who did absolutely nothing. Without making too many assumptions, I remember leaving the theater telling my boys to say their prayers for the gentleman, but I mostly remember telling them that when someone needs help it is important that we take action even if we are scared, uncomfortable, or worried about appearing obnoxious. We have a responsibility to do something. Do something for someone else in need like you would for your grandfather, your mother, or your best friend. In the end, we are all One.

Free your spirit and add a sparkle on your heart by actively being compassionate. Don't allow yourself even a moment of hesitation when you have an opportunity to help because you are actually giving yourself the greatest gift. Active compassion is your gift to be who and what you were put here to do and be.

See yourself in everyone you meet.

—Panache Desai

- ✓ **Affirmation:** I have no fear to act and to be compassionate. My spirit is free and my heart sparkles. I help others in every way possible without hesitation.

- ✓ **Action Step:** I will remind myself it is my gift and responsibility to help others. I will pay very careful attention to when I am worried about being embarrassed, perceived as obnoxious or uncertain of reaching out. When I feel these feelings I will take action anyway. I will help others in need; I will do *something*.

Being Compassionate

Feelings:

Use your feelings as a guide to which action to take. If you are feeling judgmental, annoyed, frustrated, and lonely or doing a lot of negative self-talk these are good indicators upon which to focus when using some of the tools for Being Compassionate.

Colors:

We can use color as a prompt or reminder to focus on what we have chosen. Think of the blue petal on the *Living Inspired* flower; you can wear blue, take time to look at the blue sky or blue water and remember we are all connected.

Considerations:

1. As you begin to focus on compassion, your ego may begin to tell you that people have to be held accountable and that we simply cannot help everyone. These things are true but you can still choose the way you act and think. The more you practice being compassionate the less your ego will rear its ugly head. Compassion leaves no room for anything else but our natural state of love.

2. It might feel scary or awkward to focus on compassion and to act in compassionate ways because it does leave us wide open and feeling vulnerable. When you experience these feelings remember you are building the kind of strength that is indestructible.

3. You might also think that you can't really make a difference. You may want to just continue on as is—being a good person, doing no harm; a person that will help whenever possible. If you really want to live inspired with a life full of joy and brightness, it is important for you go to the next level. Reach out, reflect, observe and keep your focus on doing and thinking as many loving things as possible. If there is one area to create the greatest life possible, this is it.

CHOICE FIVE

Living in Gratitude

> ***Gratitude bestows reverence, allowing us to encounter everyday epiphanies, transcendent moments of awe that change forever how we experience life and the world.*** —John Milton

The best way to manage a bad mood, stave off depression, attract good people and events is to be thankful. To be abundant in your thoughts and actions through gratitude is what will produce inspiration. No matter how challenging life can be it is essential to always find something for which to be thankful.

I remember one winter my daughter and I had the flu terribly. We were so sick. She was about eight years old and she was so ill that she could barely walk. We were lying in bed and she says, "Mom, the only good thing I can think of right now is that we are not throwing up." We were alive and not vomiting. Give thanks. I was grateful that she had such a mindset that was focused on the positive and not the complaining. This may sound like a small incident, but it is an illustration of how someone who lives in gratitude thinks.

Think about your own views, watch the people around you. Is their primary perspective from a place of gratitude? Gratitude is powerful; gratitude changes everything.

As you begin to live with inspiration, finding things to be grateful for will become second nature. When you practice, it becomes easy. You will even be able to give thanks during and after adversity. When bad things happen we need to feel the pain, work through it and then find the gifts that are the result.

Many people will let difficult experiences rule the rest of their lives. They become consumed with being the victim, not having enough or being good enough or believing others are not good enough. The fact is that we will live bigger brighter lives when we focus on the good gained from the bad.

Reframe to Become a Waterfall of Appreciation

We build courage, connections, strategies to share, self-confidence, compassion and resiliency through our hardships. These are some of the greatest gifts for which to be truly grateful.

It is amazing to think about all of the things that can happen and change when we practice gratitude. The most amazing outcome of gratitude is we become learners. When we can be grateful as a result of adversity we are open to more opportunities to learn and grow, even when it is hardest. We don't have to complain and whine; we can train our minds to see more than we are feeling. We should and we must honor our feelings and our sorrows. We can do this by allowing them and accepting them. When we move from complaining, self-pity and victimization toward gratitude we change our whole life and we find ways to make our greatest contributions.

If you think about some of the most challenging times in your life you find they are often later seen as times when the most learning occurred. While we learn from positive experiences too, it is our challenge to see the good in the bad. We build courage, connections, self-confidence, strategies to share, compassion and resiliency through hardships. These are some of the greatest gifts for which we can be most thankful. We determine what is most important to us and gain clarity and perspective.

Yes, it would be lovely if we lived in utopia but we don't. Your past hurts and hardships are not going anywhere; they already happened and you cannot change the past. What you *can* do is to begin to find ways to be grateful for them.

As we work through our pain we can use our thoughts to reframe without minimizing our experiences in order to move us to a new level of appreciation. The fact is we do not always have a choice in what happens to us, but we do have a choice in how we define these experiences in our life. We choose how to assimilate them in our story. I choose appreciation. Even if your ego and thought patterns are telling you that things are wrong and not possible, you can retrain and reframe how you define the past and present with your thoughts.

Some experiences may lead to the need for some professional help. It is important you seek that kind of help if you need it. But in most cases of life challenges we can use gratitude as a tool to reframe, redefine and learn from some of the worst things ever. We can turn bad to our benefit through our perceptions. Being stuck in sorrow, anger and pity only results in more of the same. When you acknowledge the bad and use it to your advantage, then you are on the path to *Living Inspired.* I visualize a massive waterfall of appreciation flowing through my life. We can be a current of gratitude.

Life will give you whatever experience is most helpful for the evolution of your consciousness.
—Eckhart Tolle

✓ **Affirmation:** I will use challenges as learning opportunities through gratitude. I allow and accept my feelings. I choose not to get stuck in self-defeating thought patterns.

✓ **Action Step:** I will practice seeing the good that comes from the bad. I know that difficult situations will always occur. I also know that I get to choose my response and that gratitude helps expand my response repertoire.

Gratitude Spot

> **It does not matter where your gratitude spot is. What matters is that you create time and space to focus on gratitude and correlating it within a space to reinforce the likelihood you will continue to practice daily.**

Living Inspired is about being intentional and proactive in how we treat ourselves, see others and navigate our lives. In order to live in gratitude it is essential to create behavioral patterns that will support gratefulness even when you are stressed or experiencing pain.

I have a chair that I use to practice generating thoughts about everything I am grateful for. You can create a spot to use as a reminder to intentionally focus on the good. As you practice, gratitude will become a way of being but during hard times or during the process of developing new thought patterns it is a good idea to create space where you can practice. It does not have to be fancy or a really big deal unless you want to do that. It can be in the car, in the shower, under your favorite tree or at the kitchen table. It does not matter where your gratitude spot is—what matters is that you create time and space to really focus on gratitude and correlating it with a space reinforces the likelihood you will practice.

When you realize there is nothing lacking the whole world belongs to you. —Lao Tsu

- ✓ **Affirmation:** I practice gratitude in everything I do and everything I think. Gratitude is my way of being and seeing.
- ✓ **Action Step:** I will create a space that I use every day to intentionally think about what I am grateful for.

Avoid the Hedonic Adaptation

Those who live in gratitude are propelled to their greatness.

When I was in college and had my first son we did not have a washer and dryer. In the big scheme of things this isn't really that big of deal but it was an inconvenience that I did not like. Now twenty-plus years later, I am grateful almost every time I do a load of laundry that I have a washer and dryer. Even if my laundry is completely out of control I am still grateful I have the opportunity to do a load. This appreciation and ongoing gratitude for my washer and dryer is how we avoid the 'hedonic adaptation' coined by researchers Sheldon and Lyubomirsky.

The hedonic adaptation is when we wish and hope for something, we are initially happier when we receive it, but we return to our old level of happiness shortly thereafter. A common example is people who win the lottery basically return to their baseline level of happiness eighteen months later.

What these researchers found is that *variety and gratitude* can keep your baseline happiness higher. So in the case of my washer and dryer, I keep being thankful that I can do a load of laundry, and maybe I keep variety by changing up my laundry systems or buying different detergents and fabric softeners. In this way I will avoid hedonic adaptation.

It sounds silly but it works and you can apply variety and gratitude to almost every area of your life to avoid the hedonic adaptation. You can do new things with your friends or partners and you can continually appreciate things about each relationship.

Another way to keep appreciation high is to think about a time when someone you loved suddenly passed away or an important relationship went awry. Didn't you wish you were more grateful when things were good? Did you wish you had done more together?

Find ways to stay present in your life and focusing on what is going well. Wake up every day with as many thank yous as you can possibly think of. Make a list of all the people, things and situations in your life that you once asked for and now are present. If your list is short, it is time for you to dig deep and start really asking for then appreciating what you want and have. These types of thought patterns and behaviors will inevitably bring more goodness into your life.

Remember, the people you see that light up a room and appear to have everything going for them are practicing *Living Inspired*. Those who live in gratitude are propelled to their greatness.

> ***Happiness is not out there for us to find. The reason that it's not out there is that it's inside us.*** —Sonja Lyubomirsky

✓ **Affirmation:** I am grateful for everything I have. I find ways to appreciate things in many different ways.

- ✓ **Action Step:** I will make a list of everything I hoped for that I have now, even things that seem trivial. I will think about ways to appreciate these things.

Thank Yous and Compliments

Cheers to making choices.

I went on a trip to Ireland. It was a trip of a lifetime with seventeen other family members. Like any robust Irish family, we are passionate people. We laugh a lot, we live fully and enthusiastically. Like any other family we have had wars and there are many harbored resentments. One thing is for certain, we all wanted to enjoy this once in a lifetime opportunity to be together and to learn about our family history.

As we embarked upon the New York airport from various places throughout the country, we were excited to see each other. We knew we all needed to do our part to intentionally keep peace, joy, forgiveness and love on our lips and in our hearts for the next ten days. My brother told me that he had decided, with his wife and two sons, to only focus on “thanks yous and compliments” during the trip to avoid arguments, annoyances, possible wars and unlimited fiascos!

I was sold immediately and coined it our mantra for the trip: *Thank Yous and Compliments*. Everyone did their part. We had the best trip possible. We laughed so hard we cried, we toasted each other, celebrated milestones, and even reconnected as a family. This may not have happened without Thank Yous and Compliments.

- The next time someone annoys you, remember to focus on Thank Yous and Compliments.
- The next time you feel yourself constricting because of resentments and past hurts, focus on Thank Yous and Compliments.
- The next time you judge or complain about that which you find upsetting, focus on Thank Yous and Compliments.

We knew no argument was worth ruining this time together. We made two simple choices: Thank Yous and Compliments. What if you choose Thanks Yous and Compliments all of the time, or at least most of the time? What beautiful moments and friendships and families could you create?

Try it today. Thank Yous and Compliments. If my wild, robust, complicated family can choose to do it, you certainly can. Cheers to making choices.

You create your own experience.

—Dr. Phil McGraw

- ✓ **Affirmation:** I find ways to be grateful. I see good in others and openly share good thoughts with them.

- ✓ **Action Step:** I will make the choice to look for things to be grateful for. I will use my energy on thoughts, ideas and emotions that widen my circle for learning.

Celebrate Your Happy Story

It is the people who can use adversity for strength and move ahead with a focus on the good that will shine the brightest.

It is just as easy to have a celebration as it is to have a gripe session. It is just as easy to compliment as it is to criticize. It is just as easy to thank someone as it is to take for granted. It is just as easy to remember all of the wonderful things in your life as it is to remember the not so good things.

Start talking about goodness. Start spreading stories of triumph and joy. The more we focus on the good the more goodness we will perpetuate. This is not a suggestion to be like an ostrich with your head in the sand; it is a suggestion to clearly and intentionally decide what you want to spread around and remember in your heart.

It is all too common for people to rehash all of the bad that has happened to them. My parents got divorced, my family has mental illness and addiction patterns, I got the fat gene, and on and on. Jack Canfield calls all this stuff we focus on the *so what*. Everyone has stuff. It is the people who can use the adversity for strength and move ahead with a focus on the good that will shine the brightest.

This may take some practice to create and spread a new story of celebration for all that has been learned, given and shared. For every bad memory and every story of hardship begin to think about a good memory and story of success. Retrain your mind so you can rewrite your story of good.

> ***Don't you know yet? It is your light that lights the world.***
> —Rumi

✓ **Affirmation:** I see the beautiful in everyday moments and share them with others. I am open-hearted and open-minded, focused on appreciation of every aspect of my life. I am grateful and joyous and I celebrate my life and others every chance I get.

✓ **Action Step:** I will intentionally talk about good things. I will find the good in every situation. I remember that I get to choose my focus and I am choosing gratitude not complaining. I will think about and write down happy memories.

Bigger Fish to Fry

You are destined for greatness and gratitude is the fastest road to your destiny.

Creating perspective for the way you live, for choosing your focus and where you put your energy is extremely important as you move along the journey of inspiration. People may try to bring you down. A heightened focus on your greatest contributions may threaten or make others feel uncomfortable.

People will try to bog you down when you begin living in gratitude because misery loves company. The bogging down may include others trying to drag you into drama or may gossip about you. They may think you have lost your marbles. These are good signs. Your mental prompt is that you have bigger fish to fry. If you get distracted by your own thoughts and feelings of being pulled away from gratitude it is important to remember you are making new choices so you can contribute more during your time on earth. When the petty stuff, daily stressors or unkind people start to infiltrate your choices remind yourself that you have *bigger fish to fry*.

It is really about keeping your eye on the prize on how you want to live your life. Stay focused on the biggest fish. You are destined for greatness and gratitude is the fastest road to your destiny.

> ***You must remain focused on your journey to greatness.*** —Les Brown

✓ **Affirmation:** I am clear on my greatest contributions and I keep a laser focus through gratitude.

✓ **Action Step:** I will remember that I have bigger fish to fry when I become distracted or stressed and lose my focus on that for which I am truly thankful.

Living in Gratitude

Feelings:

Gratitude is a choice to focus on when you are feeling stressed, discouraged, lonely, abandoned, and worried. We can use our feelings as a compass and can choose to change directions by using the tools.

Colors:

Gratitude is represented by green on the *Living Inspired* flower. Focus on green things in nature. Wear a green piece of clothing or even write with a green pen if you are focused on being more grateful.

Considerations:

1. You may feel like you are being fake or even delusional if you begin to only focus on the good things. This is a normal feeling and is part of the process. Your ego wants you to stay hung up on the bad because it is a false sense of identity. Acknowledge your feelings then take action to continue living in gratitude.

2. Living in gratitude is in no way dismissing your hardships; it is only choosing where to put your focus. Do not confuse the two.

3. Gratitude does change everything. Trust the process so you can create more good in your life.

CHOICE SIX

Focusing on Presence

Most humans are never fully present in the now because unconsciously they believe that the next moment must be more important than this one. But then you miss your whole life, which is never not now. —Eckhart Tolle

It was a pivotal moment for me when my oldest son was eighteen and leaving home. I remember the heart wrenching sobbing in the airport wondering where the time went—wondering if I had enjoyed the moments enough. Regretfully, wondering if I had been focused on the most important things and painfully knowing that much of the time I was in a distracted and stressed state of mind.

The good news is I was able to turn it around with the choices I now share and tools—all of which lead to the ultimate pathway to *Living*

Inspired through being present. It is no mistake that focusing on presence is the last choice in our journey—it is the foundation of living. No matter where you are in your life's journey you can begin focusing on presence now. Everything will change. Everything will be better than it was when you realize the moment is now—now is all we have.

His Whole Face Smiles

Presence allows us to see the beauty in others, to feel the connections all around us. It is truly the greatest gift we can give to ourselves.

It was a typical fall afternoon in the Midwest where raking leaves was a typical chore; except this day was atypical when I realized my typical was different—it was better. My son Luke and his friend Zach were helping bag the leaves. They were playing around but getting the job done. In the past, I would have acted as the task master, rushing and ordering everyone around, basically taking any bit of joy out of the task at the expense of checking it off my list. A couple of years prior I had started my *Living Inspired* journey. Peace and presence were now my focus. Simply trying to stay present and not worry that it was taking a bit longer to rake the leaves because they were horsing around, I paused and watched and laughed. Make no mistake, I was practicing and it took effort to break old habits.

Out of the blue and in moment of presence I looked over to Luke. I saw his profile. My heart melted when I saw his face. He was smiling and I realized so clearly that his whole face smiled. He glowed, joy exuded from the inside out. I was deeply grateful to have this moment, observing my son, seeing his soul shine. If I was living in my old ways of rushing, ordering others around, watching the clock, or being annoyed I would have missed one of the most beautiful moments of my life. Presence allows us to see the beauty in others, to feel the connections all around us. It is truly the greatest gift we can give to ourselves.

In your presence there is fullness of joy.
—Psalm 16:11

✓ **Affirmation:** I embrace each moment. I know the beauty of living is in the here and now. I see joy, feel connection and enjoy my life because I am present.

✓ **Action Step:** I will step back and take five deep breaths when rushing or ordering others around.

I will use self-talk to get present when I am distracted by the future or the past. I will say to help keep myself present, "See and feel what is now," or, "This is the person I love; this is the moment I have."

Make a Mantra

Mantras can help remind us that no matter where we are or how we are feeling things are always unfolding in our favor. The unfolding is the process, and everything is a process.

Focusing on presence is a continual process that will probably require many tools, especially if you are in the habit of being distracted, overachieving, con-trolling and overwhelmed. It is extremely helpful to have a few mantras or sayings to use regularly to keep you on the right track. I have two favorites:

All in Good Time
Everything is a Process.

I repeat in my mind, *everything is a Process* when I become frustrated with others or if I am uncertain about what to do or worried about an outcome or problem. It helps to remind me that no matter where I am or how I am feeling, things are always unfolding in my favor. The unfolding is the process, and everything is a process.

I repeat in my mind, *All in Good Time,* when I need to remember that everything is unfolding as it should. This mantra helps me not be so personally attached to the process. It helps me to remember that it is out of my hands and the Universe has perfect time. Both mantras bring me back to presence and when we are fully present everything else in our minds flows away. This is the process of presence in good time. This is where we begin to enjoy our lives and stop trying to control everything and everyone.

> ***In an easy and relaxed manner, in a healthy and positive way, in its own perfect time, for the highest good of all.*** —Catherine Ponder

✓ **Affirmation:** I trust the process of life and I know that everything occurs just as it should. I know and believe *everything is a Process* and occurs *All in Good Time*. I am fully present.

- ✓ **Action Step:** I will create one or two mantras that I can use to help me be present, especially when I start to feel overwhelmed, controlling or scared. I will use mantras to reteach myself how to be in the world.

Show Up

Your presence matters to others. Just as if you were to have a party or a funeral, those who show up will be remembered in your heart.

I have learned over the years of hosting baby showers, planning weddings, burying loved ones and celebrating milestones that it really matters who shows up. When we are invited to an event with people we care about we need to show up with a clean heart. The caveat here is that we don't commit to just spend time with whomever or those that don't want our best interest, we only make a very concerted effort to show up for those that we love and care about. We preserve our energy and presence for meaningful moments.

Oftentimes we get caught up in our long list of

tasks we need to get done or that we aren't in the mood. It is important to remember that our moods are usually controlled by our ego, not our spirits, so find tools to make sure you commit to show up.

I know which seats were empty at my son's wedding; I will always remember who didn't show up. I will remember when I did the same to others. I know the feeling of planning a party and feeling uneasy that people will not show, up but I also remember watching my kids wait for their classmates by the window on the day of their parties with no doubt that their whole class was coming. What happened to bring doubt and what led us to make excuses? Adults stop showing up because we become distracted by our own agendas and feelings. Your presence matters to others, just as if you were to have a party or a funeral—those who show up will be remembered in your heart.

Be the one who shows up, physically and with your mental presence. Your life will be richer and your relationships will be more meaningful. We can create the same kind of trust with others that we had as children.

> ***The key is not to prioritize what's on your schedule, but to schedule your priorities.***
>
> —Stephen Covey

- ✓ **Affirmation**: I know who is important to me and put my energy and effort in being present for them. I show up because I know my presence is a gift to others.

- ✓ **Action Step:** I will take time to clarify with whom I will spend time and then wholeheartedly show up for them. My actions and presence matter and I will do my best to align them with those I care about. I will not be distracted by others and the tasks I think I need to get done.

Open Arms, Deep Breaths and Heart Centered Hands

Use your body to your advantage; listen to it and let it help you manage your mind.

Our bodies can be messengers and remind us of how we are feeling. When we become stressed or distracted we often clench and tense up. When we are overstimulated or overwhelmed we are constricted in our thoughts, actions and body movements. When we are constricted we are not present and we are not open to all of the possibilities before us.

A good tool when you feel you are not in the moment is to use your body to bring your mind back to the here and now. Wherever you are, open your arms wide. If you can walk around or step outside with your arms spread open, palms flat and facing up and take a few deep breaths you will feel the stress and constriction release. Your mind will open back up to the moment and you will be back on the path of presence.

If you are feeling angry, frustrated or lonely bring your palms together on the center of your chest or lay your hands on your heart and take a few deep breaths. This will bring you to a place of compassion and presence. Use your body to your advantage; listen to it and let it help you manage your mind.

If you cannot do these movements at the exact moment you are feeling out of the present then you can mentally repeat: *Open arms, heart centered hands and breathe.* You can coach your mind to relax and get centered if you use this tool regularly.

Breath is the link between mind and body.

—Dan Brule

- ✓ **Affirmation**: My body helps my mind and my mind helps my body. I keep them in sync to focus on presence.
- ✓ **Action Step**: The next time I feel stressed or distracted or constricted in anyway, I will use my body to help me focus on being present.

Be Interested, Not Interesting

When we stop making things about ourselves we become more interested in others which leads to the reciprocal connection that we all long for.

If you want high quality relationships and you want to attract the right people into your life it is essential to be a good listener—a listener that is present. A listener that isn't worried about what they are going to say next or tell a story about them in relation to what the other person is saying. A good listener won't interrupt, judge or think about other things when someone is talking to them.

Being present is more than making eye contact. It's about showing up for another with an open heart and clear mind. The only way we have a clear mind is to be in the present moment. When we stop making things about ourselves we become more interested in others which leads to reciprocal connections.

This practice is such a gift to others because they will feel valued and accepted by you. It is such a gift to you because you will learn from others, realize those to intentionally spend time with, and your heart will sparkle with compassion. Without presence we will never be more interested than trying to be interesting.

> ***Listening is being completely present to whatever is before us with all of who we are.***
>
> —Mark Nepo

✓ **Affirmation:** I listen with an open heart and clear mind. Helping people feel valued and accepted is aligned with my values. I am more interested in others than trying to be interesting. I am present and want to learn.

✓ **Action Step:** I will practice being present with an open heart and clear mind. I will stop myself if I try to interrupt, interject or wander off in my thoughts when someone is talking with me.

Idea Book and To-Do Book

Empty your mind. Make space for ideas and possibilities. Plant the seed in your mind that you can generate new ideas.

How many times have you been in the grocery store repeating in your mind over and over what you need to get and then get home to realize you forgot what you went for? How often do you walk into a room and can't remember why you went there in the first place? When was the last time you actually came up with a new idea? When was the last time you came up with any idea, not even a good one?

I often think we are in a new idea epidemic. Our minds are so bogged down with thoughts of what we need to do and our lives are so full of stimuli that we have forgotten how to step back, pause, reflect and generate new thoughts and ideas. We are too often in reactive states rather than proactive states.

One tool you can use is to write down things you need to remember. Use this as a strategy to empty your mind, to create space for new ideas, solutions, and ways of living.

I carry two journals with me. One is my to-do

book; it is full of work tasks and family and household logistics. The other is my idea book; things I want to do, books I want to read, something interesting that someone mentioned, quotes I heard and love, new ideas and possibilities that come to mind. I record beautiful moments, places I have visited, and other thoughts in my idea book.

When I first started using a little book to write my to-dos down I put everything in it including ideas. This works as long as you are emptying your mind and using your book as a reference. In addition, it is important to write down your ideas right away because it has been proven that if you don't, you won't remember them.

Empty your mind, make space for ideas and possibilities. Plant the seed in your mind that you can generate new ideas. We are all full of possibilities but those possibilities are dwindled when our minds are overflowing with to-dos.

> ***My ideas usually come not at my desk writing but in the midst of living.*** —Anais Nin

- ✓ **Affirmation:** I have many new ideas that are full of creativity, innovation and joy.

- ✓ **Action Step:** I will write down my to-dos and ideas in order to keep my mind clear and open to the possibilities.

Mini Meditations
& Purposeful Prayer

Prayer is a platform to share what is on your mind. Meditation is a platform to clear your mind to receive answers. Both are necessary in the process of learning presence.

We don't have to be gurus and devout human beings in order to be guided by a higher power. Like getting our minds empty we also need to get prepared to be receptive to our greatest contributions and gifts. Practice being quiet and the answers will come. Prayer is a platform to share what is on your mind. Meditation is a platform to clear your mind and listen. Both are necessary in the process of learning presence.

A few things I do to help myself focus on presence are:

- Begin each prayer with gratitude for what is. Then ask questions or ask for what I may need support with, especially if I am worried about someone else and more particularly my children. Having faith is an important part of purposefully praying. For example, "Dear God, I trust you. I know everything is a process unfolding in my favor. Thank you for my faith and for all of the good in my life. Right now I am worried and I am reaching out to practice increasing my faith. Please help me with…"

- Take a one minute vacation. This is a great exercise to get centered and back in the present through creating a peaceful state of mind. Set a timer for a minute. Close your eyes and take a few deep breaths. Visualize yourself on vacation, think about what you see, what you hear, and how you feel.

- Four Breaths: Breathe in for four seconds, hold it for four seconds, and breathe out for four seconds. Repeat four times. When we stop to breathe we are creating space for presence. When you are counting and breathing it helps keep you in the moment rather than your mind wandering.

Meditation and prayer are keys to presence. You can practice and even become quite dedicated in both spiritual practices like many others have. It is certainly a good idea. Or you can just take moments here and there to do mini-meditations and say purposeful prayers to help you practice focusing on presence. The most important thing to remember is that you don't have to force either one; there is no perfection and you are right where you are supposed to be. Relax.

> ***Be happy in the moment, that's enough. Each moment is all we need, not more.***
>
> —Mother Teresa

- ✓ **Affirmation:** I listen to find my presence. I am guided by all that is good and powerful.
- ✓ **Action Step:** I will take time to stop and pause. I will listen to guidance beyond this world. I will exercise my faith and ground it in gratitude through prayer and meditation.

Focusing on Presence

Feelings:

Presence is the central force in *Living Inspired.* If you are feeling misguided, confused, distracted, reactive, too busy, unhappy or unfulfilled putting a focus on stopping, pausing and breathing will help you get centered in the life you are meant to live.

Colors:

When we use tools to help us to remember to stop and pause, like breathing or a song or a happy memory, we can also use colors. The purple petal on the *Living Inspired* flower represents presence. Purple is rich and has depth just as presence does.

Considerations:

1. Learning to live in the moment does not happen overnight. Most of us will continue to get distracted, stressed or feel like hamsters spinning in a wheel. Focusing on presence is a tool to get back on the path of peace faster. It is not intended to make your life or you 'perfect.'

2. We don't have to make being present complicated. It doesn't have to be some big search to become enlightened. It's doing little things that can make a big difference. There are few people in the history of the world who are truly enlightened. Don't worry, we don't have to be one of them.

3. The less you pressure yourself the better things will become in your life. It's when we forget who we are at our core that we get

into living miserably or in mediocrity. Presence helps to remind you why you are here and what you have to give.

CONCLUSION

Make *IT* Happen, Rosie!

Living Inspired is when we are in a state of mind to receive the gifts all around us then share them with others through our actions, our energy and our contributions. We focus on living a life that inspires others and we help them see they, too, can be who they are meant to be and discover the contributions they are here to make.

One day I received a mass email from the Cincinnati Reds baseball team that there were cheap seats open and 'Credence Clearwater Revived' was playing after the game. My husband and I were not in a happy place within our marriage. We were both annoyed with one another and were in a solid downward spiral for months and even possibly for years. I had a thought that it might be a good idea for us to have a getaway. He loved the Reds and I loved Credence.

The night before we were to leave we had a huge fight so I didn't even want to go to the game anymore. We barely talked on the long, quiet three-hour drive. As we arrived at the All American Ballpark in Cincinnati music was playing. We got our hotdogs and drinks and proceeded to the nose bleed section. Sitting in front us were Rosie and her grandfather. Sitting in front of us were two angels that will forever stay with us and one of the best gifts we ever received.

Rosie was a dedicated Reds fan. She wore a red t-shirt with every player and their number handwritten with sharpie on the back in what looked to be like a third grader's writing. She was enthusiastic, to say the least. She would jump up and scream every time anything exciting happened or when her favorite players were up to bat. Periodically she would look at us like she was a tad apologetic, but I reassured her that it was fine and that we were the right people to be excited around. We didn't care if she was blocking our view or distracting us from the game; her vibrancy was entertainment enough. Her grandfather sat quietly. I am sure he was as a dedicated fan as Rosie; more reserved but just as intense. The most beautiful dance between them was one of the greatest blessings.

Rosie was eating pizza and the red sauce was all over her face. Her grandfather pulled a paper towel from his pocket and handed it to her. He never ordered her to clean up or be neat. He never said a word. Rosie would jump up and down, walk down the three stairs to the railing and walk back over and over again. Her grandfather never told her to sit down or to be quiet. He completely accepted Rosie. He let her be who she was.

Rosie would scream—really scream—at the players. Sometimes when she would scream she would just reach out and put her hand over her grandfather's ear to protect him from the sound. Not because he was annoyed or told her to be quiet, but because Rosie had consideration for him. A consideration that wasn't dictated; it was consideration from the purest love.

As the game progressed things were getting super intense. We watched Rosie and her grandfather and it became apparent that a Red's win was serious business for them. The game had gone into two extra innings. Rosie's grandfather sat quietly and intently biting his finger nails every so often. Rosie's anticipation and energy was off the charts. She could no longer sit, not even for a moment. She was standing at the railing—it was the time for the winning hit to take place.

Rosie's grandfather sat in his chair as Rosie stood on the landing and leaned on the railing staring intently at the batter. Her grandfather said firmly and assuredly, "Rosie, Make IT happen.

Make IT happen, Rosie." She looked at him and nodded her head with complete confirmation.

The batter hits the ball—the Reds win! As they are running the bases, collecting their points, everyone is yelling and celebrating. Amidst the excitement, I look at Rosie as she smiles and nods at her grandfather confirming that she *Made IT Happen.* Without a doubt in her mind and without a doubt in her grandfather's mind, Rosie was responsible for the win.

As we left the ball park that day, I mentioned to my husband how awesome it was to watch Rosie and her grandfather. My husband responded, "I want to be more like Rosie's grandfather." He wanted to be accepting, present, joyous and empowering. I wanted to be the same—don't we all? Sometimes when we see it in others we can discover what we want. When we practice these things we can help others see them for themselves. *This is when we are amazing.*

We can be what we want to be by using the tools and making bright choices to live inspired. Let us show up for ourselves and others. Let us create joy. Let us be considerate—be compassionate.

Let's live in gratitude and practice courage. Let's be present.

You can be amazing.

Make *IT* Happen!

ABOUT THE AUTHOR

ERIN RAMSEY

Erin Ramsey is a nationally recognized inspirational speaker with over twenty years of service in the public sector. She earned a Bachelor of Arts degree in Child Development and Psychology and a Master of Sciences in Public Service Administration.

Erin is married to her high school sweetheart and is the mother of three sons and a daughter. She loves to read, walk labyrinths, entertain and bring people together for empowerment.

Visit **www.erinramsey.com** to follow Erin's blog, order *Living Inspired* products or to connect with her on social media. If you are interested in inviting Erin to facilitate a retreat, doing a keynote address, a workshop or strategic planning session, she can be reached at: erin@erinramsey.com. She would love to hear what you are doing to *Be Amazing*! See the following pages for *Living Inspired* products by Erin Ramsey.

Living Inspired
Products by Erin Ramsey

- ***Be Amazing* Workbook & Guide to Starting a POW WOW**

Living an amazing life does not need to be complicated, but knowing how to make it happen and actually doing it may be two different things. The *Be Amazing* Workbook is intended to help you jumpstart and encourage you on your path to *Living Inspired* as you move from the space of knowing to doing. The tools in *Be Amazing* are simple and easy to use but require practice. The activities in the workbook provide strategies that will guide you in practicing using the tools. The workbook can be used and studied alone or with a group of people you trust. It also includes a guide on how to start a POW WOW. A POW WOW is a group of cool women coming together to learn and to grow. A POW WOW goes way beyond bunco and book club. Become a part of the POW WOW Movement!

The POW WOWs are not to be about our roles; rather it is about our spirits. We need to help ourselves so we can help others. —Erin Ramsey

- **Jar of Possibilities**

This is a unique tool that Erin makes by hand with her family that is designed to help people talk, think and write about their memories, ideas and experiences.

The jar contains thirty-nine prompts that can be used in solitude for journaling, with family and friends around the dinner table, at parties, during staff meetings or anywhere you need to spread good energy, connect with others and focus on possibilities. They make great gifts, too!

The **Jar of Possibilities** is currently available in Erin's ETSY Shop at this link: **https://www.etsy.com/shop/LivingInspiredLLC?ref=hdr_shop_menu**

- ***Be Amazing* Workshops & Webinars**

Get connected with others who are on the journey to Living Inspired!

Check Erin Ramsey's website for more upcoming opportunities. **www.erinramsey.com**

Made in the USA
San Bernardino, CA
27 April 2016